# BOOK ANALYSIS

Written by Cécile Perrel and Florence Balthasar

Translated by Ciaran Traynor

AF131384

# Brodeck's Report

## BY PHILIPPE CLAUDEL

# PHILIPPE CLAUDEL

## FRENCH WRITER AND DIRECTOR

- **Born in Dombasle-sur-Meurthe (France) in 1962.**
- **Notable works:**
  - *Grey Souls* (2003), novel
  - *Monsieur Linh and His Child* (2005), novel
  - *Petite fabrique des rêves et des réalités* ("The Making of Dreams and Realities", 2008), novel

Philippe Claudel is a French writer and director. He is also a senior lecturer at the University of Nancy and a professor at the European Audiovisual and Cinema Institute. He has taught prisoners and disabled people. He is also the author of more than 20 books, which have been translated into dozens of languages and won many awards, including *Grey Souls*, *Monsieur Linh and His Child* and *Brodeck's Report*. Claudel's first film, *I've Loved You So Long*, came out in 2008. The theme of war and its consequences can be found in several of his works.

# BRODECK'S REPORT

## A WAR MEMOIR

- **Genre**: novel
- **Reference edition**: Claudel, P. (2010) *Brodeck's Report*. Trans. Cullen, J. London: Quercus.
- **1st edition**: 2007
- **Themes**: Second World War, murder, fear, madness, investigation, memoire

*Brodeck's Report* was published in 2007. It is about a man named Brodeck, who lives in a remote village. One day, the only foreigner in the village is murdered by some of the other villagers. As Brodeck is the only one who both can type and has a typewriter, he is asked to write a precise, detailed report to prove that there was nothing illegal about the death. However, he was not there when it happened, and so he begins to gather information. The reader follows him in this task, which is broken up every so often by his memories of being a prisoner in a concentration camp during the Second World War (1939-1945). Brodeck has to write about the unspeakable and asks himself questions about the true face of human nature.

# SUMMARY

## WAR WOUNDS

Brodeck lives in a little mountain village with his family: his wife Emélia, their daughter Poupchette and Fédorine, an old woman who looked after him when he was a child. He met his wife while he was studying in the town of S. thanks to the residents of his village. At the time, they all clubbed together to send someone to university, and Brodeck was the most gifted.

Soon, rumours about the gathering of troops at the border began to circulate, and workers' demonstrations broke out in town. However, Brodeck did not take part. One night, there was a riot: the shops belonging to the *Fremdër* ("foreigners", "traitors" or "filth") were vandalised. Brodeck even looked on, helpless and outraged, as an old man was killed. He then went to Emélia's house to her to marry him, and the two escaped the town to take refuge in the village. As a result, he abandoned his studies.

Some time after start of the war, an enemy troop called the *Fratergekeime*, led by Captain Buller, came to the village. At first, living with the army was very difficult for the villagers. Buller demanded the "cleansing" of the village. He insisted so much that the mayor, as well as several other important men in the village, wrote down the names of the only two villagers who were born elsewhere: Brodeck and Simon Frippman. Both of them were arrested and separated. Brodeck was sent to a camp, where he was treated like an animal. A man was chosen at random each day in the camp to be publicly hanged to please the director's wife. Brodeck therefore lived in constant fear, not knowing whether he would survive. When he returned, he was unable to tell anyone except Fédorine about the horrors he had gone through.

While Brodeck was imprisoned, Emélia was also scarred by the war. One day, three young girls who were clearly on the run were found in the forest and taken to the soldiers. Emélia, who had come to their defence, was imprisoned with them, and the soldiers did with them as they pleased. The next day, Fédorine found the three young girls dead: they had all been raped and tortured, by both the soldiers and some villagers. Only Emélia survived, but the experience scarred her. She retreated into silence, and even her husband's return was not enough to restore her voice. Emélia gave birth to Poupchette as a result of the rape, and Brodeck recognised her as his daughter and loved her with all his heart.

## THE MURDER OF THE FOREIGNER

The war is finally over. One night, as he is going into Schloss' inn, Brodeck walks in on the other men of the village, who have just committed a murder. They have killed the man known as the *Anderer* (or "the Other"), a foreigner who had come to live in the village a short time before.

The villagers make the collective decision to ask Brodeck to write a report (for the village's archives) on what has just happened, so that they are not judged and it will be clear that they acted within their rights. The *Anderer* had made the residents feel uncomfortable and unsettled the balance of the village with his taciturn, mannered and observant presence and attitude. They completely rejected him, unable to cope with his brutally honest descriptions of them which revealed their hidden flaws. In spite of his disgust with the villagers, Brodeck has no choice but to accept. Brodeck describes his childhood in parallel with the story of the village crime, which he calls the *Ereigniës* (meaning "the thing that happened"). He tells us about his childhood, his life with Fédorine, his arrival in the village, his studies in S., his meeting with Emélia, his return to the village, the war and the hell he was put through in the camp.

The day after the tragedy, Brodeck begins to gather information in order to write his Report. The *Anderer* arrived in the village one day in May, dressed in eccentric clothes that made him stand out in the simple setting, along with his horse, Mademoiselle Julie, and his donkey, Monsieur Socrate. The other villagers immediately distrusted and feared him. Since the end of the war, no foreigner had come to the village. Brodeck, on the other hand, was happy to see a new face. However, the *Anderer*'s habits were not appreciated by the other villagers from the very beginning. He had very strange mannerisms, took an excessive interest in his appearance and behaved very unusually, particularly with his animals, which he treated like real men.

Brodeck is quick to realise that the men of the village had agreed to meet on the night of the murder and wonders why he was not invited. It turns out that Brodeck has frightened the other villagers since he came back from the camp, partly because they feel guilty about their involvement in the hell he had to live through, and partly because the terrible experience of the camps means that he is no longer like the others. Their guilt spills over onto paper when the *Anderer* makes several portraits of the villagers, which he displays at Schloss' inn one day. This is the event which sets everything off: the residents could no longer bear the presence of this foreigner.

Shortly after beginning his Report, Brodeck realises that someone has been in the room he types in. The room used to belong to Brodeck's friend Diodème, the village teacher of the village. The intruder has turned the place upside down trying to find his documents, but was unsuccessful. It is at this point that Brodeck discovers a letter to him from Diodème hidden in a drawer. The teacher died several weeks ago in mysterious circumstances. The letter turns out to be a confession: Diodème explains why Brodeck was arrested and sent to the camp.

During his investigation to discover the exact circumstances of the death of the *Anderer*, Brodeck discovers that the mayor had asked the foreigner to leave the village, which he did not do. A few days later, the *Anderer*'s horse and donkey were found drowned in the river, their legs bound together. His own death followed just two days later. By going over the events, Brodeck therefore makes the connection and discovers the reason for the murder: the *Anderer* had revealed the villagers' hidden faces in the portraits he had made of them.

Once his work is finished, Brodeck gives it to Orschwir, the mayor. The man burns it, claiming that memory can be an extremely dangerous thing. Brodeck is no longer able to live among these men, who he has made uncomfortable since he returned from the camp, and he decides to leave the village with Fédorine, Emélia and Poupchette.

# CHARACTER STUDY

## BRODECK

Even though Brodeck is the main character of the story, we are never told his full name, his age, or even his nationality. However, we can assume that he is around 30, since he has had the time to go to university, get married and return to live in the village.

He is an orphan who Fédorine found in a ruined house, in a country which is never identified. Fédorine decided to take him in, and the two moved to the village, where they both still live.

Brodeck proved to be academically gifted and was sent to the University of S. by the rest of the village. This is where he met Emélia, his future wife. However, the war threw a spanner in the works. Since he comes from a foreign country, he was deported to a concentration camp, where he was treated like an animal. He was forced to behave like a dog, walking on all fours, wearing a collar and a leash, and eating out of a bowl: the guards called him "Brodeck-the-Dog" (Chapter 38). However, Brodeck managed to survive this torture and return to the village.

In spite of this horrific experience, Brodeck is not bitter and does not judge people. He is an extremely sensitive, wise man. He has learned to observe and interpret human behaviour. He uses common sense to explain the *Anderer*'s death, and his Report is based on the facts: "I have kept it simple. I have tried to tell the story faithfully. I have not made anything up. I have not altered anything". While gathering information for his Report (and when the fruit of his labour is burned), he realises that he too scares and upsets the villagers. He therefore decides to leave the village to be able to finally live his life.

## THE *ANDERER*

The *Anderer* is a man who it is difficult to put an age to. He has blond curly hair, a childlike face and round cheeks:

> "He always had a big smile on his face, a smile that often substituted for words, which he tended to use sparingly. He had beautiful, jade-green eyes, very round and slightly bulging, which made his look even more penetrating."

His appearance upsets the villagers because he does not dress like them: he wears embroidered clothes made out of expensive material.

Nobody knows his name or why he chose to move to this specific village. He spends his time drawing and taking notes in a little notebook, which makes the villagers nervous, as they feel like he is spying on them. One day, Brodeck overhears a conversation which heralds the approaching tragedy: "Maybe you're right [...] maybe that notebook should never go anywhere. Or maybe the person it belongs to is the one who cannot leave, not ever".

Although he lives in the village, the *Anderer* lives apart and does not mix with the others. However, he occasionally speaks with Brodeck, who, feeling he can trust him for some reason, tells him what happened to him and Emélia.

The general curiosity he arouses in the villagers slowly morphs into hatred. The displaying of the portraits is the final straw: they are too painfully close to the truth for the villagers to accept. They expose their real faces: "they said [...] things that should never have been said, and they revealed truths that had been carefully smothered".

## FÉDORINE

Fédorine took Brodeck in at the age of four, when he had just lost his parents. She looked after him like a mother and took him far from his ruined house and his dead parents. It is impossible to say how old she is, and Brodeck even says:

> "I do not know if Fédorine was ever young. I have always seen her twisted and bent [...] Even when I was a small child and she took me in, she already looked like a battered old witch."

When he returns from the camp, she is the one who looks after him. She knows remedies and potions to ease sickness and fever. She is also the one who takes care of Poupchette, since Emélia, traumatised by what has happened, is in no position to be a mother. She trusts Brodeck with her life, but does not involve herself with the villagers, since she is extremely distrustful of them.

## EMÉLIA

Emélia is Brodeck's wife. She met him while he was studying in S., where she worked as an embroiderer. She married him and went with him to his village when the war broke out.

She is extremely beautiful, and it is thanks to his memories of her that Brodeck resisted in the camp and found the courage to survive hell. The war also left her with scars: after courageously defending three young girls who were raped by soldiers, she was also raped and left for dead. After this assault, she gave birth to a little girl called Poupchette.

Because of this experience, she loses the ability to speak and stops communicating with people. However, she seems to come back to life a little at the end of the novel, as the family prepare to leave the village. She squeezes her husband's neck, as if to encourage him to leave forever this place where they have lived through so much horror and where the people they lived with betrayed them. This is an undeniable sign that she is heartened by the thought of leaving.

## THE VILLAGERS

The villagers seem to form a little homogenous group; they are a character as much as Brodeck or Emélia are. They act together, as a unit, which can seem quite oppressive at times. However, there are a few men who stand out:

- **Diodème, the villager teacher and Brodeck's friend**. At the beginning of the book we find out that he died three weeks ago: he probably committed suicide. He was never able to forgive himself for betraying Brodeck to the soldiers in the village. Brodeck finally learns the truth of his arrest from a letter written by Diodème. He was a good man. He was not at the *Ereigniës*, since he was away from the village when it happened.

- **Hans Orschwir, the village mayor**. He took part in the *Ereigniës* and explains to Brodeck what he wants from his Report. He considers himself to be the protector of the peace in the village. He often speaks in metaphors. For example, he compares men to the pigs that he raises:

> "They're capable of eating their own brothers, their own flesh. It wouldn't bother them at all – to them, it's all the same. [...] Because they eat everything, Brodeck, without question. And they don't think, Brodeck, not them. They know nothing of remorse. They live. The past is unknown to them. They've got the right idea, don't you think?"

- Orschwir is among those who collaborated with the enemy when the village was occupied. He says on several occasions that memory is a poison which must be extracted, which is why he burns Brodeck's Report.
- **Göbbler, Brodeck's nearest neighbour**. Göbbler watches his neighbour at night while he types up his Report. When the village was occupied by enemy troops, he convinced the villagers that there were positive aspects to the occupation and become a sort of second mayor. He was often in the tent of Adolf Buller, the captain of the group of soldiers stationed in the village. When the three young girls on the run were brought to him, he made the decision to hand them over to the enemy, while knowing

full well that he was signing their death warrant. He is an evil man with no scruples whatsoever.

- **Dieter Schloss, the owner of the biggest bar in the village, Schloss' inn**. In spite of the fact that there are virtually never any travellers, the inn still has four rooms, one of which is occupied by the *Anderer* during his stay in the village. The inn is also the place where the unmentionable incident happened: the *Anderer's* murder. During the book, Schloss turns out to be just like most of the villagers: a follower, or perhaps even an opportunist, but not truly evil: "I did what I was told, that's all. I don't want any trouble [...] I'm just a simple man [...] but I'm not the worst, you know". The innkeeper confesses to Brodeck twice. The second time, he recounts a conversation he overheard between the *Anderer* and the mayor. This account makes Brodeck realise that the villagers were already harbouring threatening thoughts and feelings against the *Anderer* before his murder.

# ANALYSIS

## A UNIVERSAL NOVEL

It is not easy to write a universal novel which moves everyone. The writer must go beyond their own cultural sensitivity and conceptions of the world to create a book that everyone can relate to. Claudel manages to accomplish this difficult task with *Brodeck's Report*.

### Undefined spatial and temporal elements

In order to achieve this goal, the author uses a very simple technique: he keeps the reader in the dark about the places and time when his story is set. When place names or elements of the scenery appear in the story, they are all made up by the author. For example, the Staubi river and the mountains which can be seen on the horizon, as well as the Hunterpitz and the three Schnikelkopf, are all fictional. Claudel also chooses to reduce the name of the main town to its simplest expression: a single letter, S. He also simply omits certain pieces of information, such as the name of the village. The haziness of the spatial and temporal information we are given is the novel's main accomplishment: if it is not located anywhere, it can be located everywhere. The same is true of the time frame: there is never any mention of the date. The story can therefore be applied to any place and any time.

However, there are several clues in the story which allow us to unconsciously specify the location:

- The mountainous environment and the old Germanic-sounding language restrict the setting to central Europe.
- The description of the *Fratergekeime* immediately makes us think of the Nazi soldiers who denied Brodeck's humanity by treating him like an animal when he was imprisoned in the camp. The narrator describes them in the following terms:

> "... men very much like us. Having gone to university in their Capital, I happened to know them well. We associated with some of them since they often visited our village [...] and spoke a language which is the twin sister of our own and which we understand with little difficulty."

- The capital where Brodeck studied is simply called S. However, this could also be a clue: in the 1920s, the Nazi government set up its headquarters in Stuttgart, a former Central European capital.
- The *Pürische Nacht*, the revolt which Brodeck witnessed in S., has more than a few things in common with the Night of Broken Glass (9-10 November 1938), a day and night of anti-Jewish rioting, pillaging, destruction and lynching which took place simultaneously across Nazi Germany. Many Jewish shops and places of worship were ransacked.

These indications seem to anchor the book in Nazi Germany: the hatred of foreigners, war and collaboration; the vandalism; the German-sounding language; the camps; and so on. However, Claudel admitted that he did not want to write "a book about the Holocaust, there are already thousands of them. *Brodeck's Report* takes place in Eastern Europe, that's as precise at it gets. French people will be inclined to think that it is set in Alsace, because of the dialect that I invented. However, some of my German friends thought of Austria. The former Yugoslavia also comes to mind..."[1] (Leménager, *Philippe Claudel: Le Rapport de Brodeck est une parabole sur la Shoah,* 2007). Here, the author confirms his desire to write a universal book, and not to concentrate on a particular event. For him, a "historical thesis disguised as a novel" (ibid.) is uninteresting: you might as well buy a real book of documented history.

## The village: a microcosm of society

The author therefore does not completely lift the veil of mystery. To make his story universal, Claudel uses another technique: he creates a microcosm of society in the village to portray society as a whole.

Village life, and life in society as a whole, is broken up into three time periods:

- **Before the war**, in spite of their isolation, the villagers are welcoming. Travellers are greeted warmly in the inn: they bring a breath of fresh air which makes the village come to life. Those who wish to stay longer are taken in with open arms, like Fédorine and Brodeck: "They settled us in the cabin and made it clear that we could stay there for one night or for several years". After all, "back in those days, people were not yet afraid of strangers, even when they were the poorest of the poor".

---

1. This quotation has been translated by BrightSummaries.com.

- **During the war**, fear replaces their former solidarity: the occupants command and the villagers obey. It is better to sacrifice a few for the survival and peace of the rest of the village. All it takes is one person, Göbbler, to sing the praises of the occupiers to convince those with doubts. As a result, they denounce Brodeck and Frippman, who they previously treated like brothers.
- **After the war**, the scars do not fade: the air is still laden with suspicion and those who are different are viewed with mistrust. Brodeck is watched and kept at a distance; in reality, he is simply tolerated in a village where "memory was destined to weigh heavily for centuries to come" because of the horror of the camps and their collaboration, just like the rest of the population which did nothing during the conflict. The *Anderer*'s arrival is now greeted in a manner that is far from spontaneous or welcoming. Moreover, the fact that he is different makes him the perfect target.

Through this, the reader begins to understand what causes a society to behave and react the way it does through life in the village. We could therefore be in any village, with any villagers – described here as a crowd, following the herd without asking too many questions – any opportunistic leaders, like Orschwir and Göbbler, and any victims, like Brodeck and the *Anderer*.

## MEMORY AND GUILT

When the war comes to an end in the novel, a monument to the fallen villagers is erected in the village square. Brodeck's name is also on inscribed on it, since he is still imprisoned in the camp. This seems to pacify the villagers and assuage their guilt. They may have committed a terrible act in denouncing him and sending him to a camp, but they honour his memory by writing his name on the monument. However, the villagers are unaware that Brodeck has survived. When he returns to the village, clearly still alive, they are forced to erase his name, and resentment slowly begins to take root in their hearts. His death would have allowed them to be at peace with themselves: they believed that building a monument was enough to erase their sins. However, Brodeck's return forces them to face their betrayal once again. Brodeck is a mirror reflecting the villagers' baseness, and he is therefore rejected.

Consequently, we notice that memory is considered to be something negative: it must be neutralised, because nothing good can come of it. This is confirmed by the mayor when he tells Brodeck that:

> "Everything that belongs to yesterday belongs to death, and the important thing is to live. I know you are well aware of that, Brodeck – you came back from a place people don't come back from [...] The flock counts on me to protect it from every danger, and of all dangers, memory is one of the most terrible."

Forgetting seems to be key to living a happy life.

The desire to write up a report follows the same logic: the villagers want it to ease their conscience, but once it is finished, they prefer to get rid of it and free themselves from this overwhelming memory. Brodeck, however, cannot forget, which is why he chooses to leave the village.

## A MULTIFACETED STYLE OF WRITING

### Personal and poetic

In keeping with the novel's universality, the author's writing style irresistibly draws the reader into a story which they cannot completely disassociate themselves from: the reader becomes very attached to Brodeck, because they are given intimate access to his thoughts. This painful story of a wasted life grabs our attention and moves us deeply. There are several writing techniques which create this effect:

- **The use of the first person singular**. Choosing to write the book in the first person singular propels the reader into the heart of the story. We therefore find ourselves the confidants of the protagonist and have a privileged view into his personal life. Consequently, the reader establishes a familiar relation with the narrator, who becomes a close friend. Moreover, this "I" contrasts with the crowd, with the mass of others, which strengthens the bond between the reader and this particular individual.
- **The structure**. This personal tone is combined with the writing of Brodeck's "intimate book". His Report is a sort of autobiography in which he tells his story, combining a range of shocking events from the past and present. For him, the story reflects his life: "If my tale looks like some monstrous body, that is because it is made in the image of my life, which I have been unable to contain, which is going to wrack and ruin".

- **The appearance of memories**. Memories reappear suddenly, bouncing off each other and mixing to create a sort of "jumble".

> "When I read the pages of my account thus far, I see that I move around with my words like tracked game on the run, sprinting, zig-zagging, trying to throw the dogs and hunters in hot pursuit off the scent. This jumble contains everything. I am emptying my life into it. Writing is relief to both my heart and my stomach."

Faced with this hesitant confession, the reader can neither remain indifferent nor distance himself. The author therefore draws out the almost intimate link between his character and the readers.

In spite of his extremely difficult life, Brodeck still manages to find beauty in the world. He waxes lyrical about nature and scenery, the childish vitality of little Poupchette and the silent beauty of his wife Emélia.

Brodeck even manages to see the beauty in horror. During the *Pürische Nacht* in S., Brodeck "could not help imagining that someone had scattered precious stones by the handful all through the Kolesh quarter. The thought gave the small street a new dimension, sparkling, marvelous, like the setting of a fairytale". These precious stones are none other than the broken glass of the "shop windows that gaped like the jaws of dead animals". The camps which "had sprung up all over the place on the other side of the border [are] like poisonous flowers".

Poetry is interwoven with horror, not to mitigate it or make it more palatable, but to underline it and make it all the more shocking. However, it is useless "in the matter of [...] survival".

## Communicating a message

For Claudel, memory must be kept alive: it must not fade. His novel sometimes recalls the terrifying account of Primo Levi (Italian writer, 1919-1987), *If This Is a Man*, which tells the story of his imprisonment in Auschwitz. Humanity must certainly remember, but Claude does not set out to condemn or insist that this should never happen again: he simply tries to write a story to help men to understand men. More than remembering a precise traumatic event, the author wants to highlight that the past in general must not be forgotten.

The story switches constantly between the present, with Brodeck's life in the village and the writing of the Report, and his memories from the war and his survival in the camp. The character's thoughts allow us to see events in a new light, to understand or at least try to understand men and what pushes them to act in a certain way, do each other harm or come to each other's aid.

He therefore shows that warmth and goodness can appear at any moment, even in the worst of situations. This is exactly the message he conveys when Brodeck was returning home from the camp. On the way, he met a man who offered him hospitality, without asking any questions. "'Do not speak,' he said. 'I'm not going to ask any questions. I do not know exactly where you have come from, but I think I can guess'". The man even gave him clothes so he could return to the village: "They are just your size. They belonged to my son, but he won't be coming back. It is no doubt better that way." We understand the implication that the man's son was probably one of the torturers and that his father would prefer that he was dead rather than have to live with this burden.

Claudel's novel is anything but a condemnation of humanity and its actions: it is rather an interrogation on human nature and the relationship men have with their own memory and with what they do not know.

# FURTHER REFLECTION

## SOME QUESTIONS TO THINK ABOUT...

- What are the similarities and differences between *Brodeck's Report* and other works on the same theme? What makes Claudel's novel original? Justify your answer.
- Describe the character of the *Anderer*. Why did the villagers murder him?
- In your opinion, is there a link between the *Anderer* and Brodeck? What kind of link? Explain your answer.
- Why is Brodeck disappointed by the attitude of the former schoolmaster, Limmat?
- What can we say about the innkeeper, Schloss? How does Brodeck see him?
- Brodeck claims that, although he was the one who was coming home, it was Diodème who could finally live. Comment on this.
- "My name is Brodeck and I had nothing to do with it." Comment on this sentence which opens and closes the novel.
- What conception of memory does the novel convey?
- In your opinion, does Claudel have an optimistic or pessimistic view of man in general?
- Besides man, the novel reflects on several concepts. In your opinion, how is fear portrayed? What about God?

*We want to hear from you!*
*Leave a comment on your online library*
*and share your favourite books on social media!*

# FURTHER READING

## REFERENCE EDITION

- Claudel, P. (2010) *Brodeck's Report*. Trans. Cullen, J. London: Quercus.

## REFERENCE STUDIES

- Aarons, V. ed. (2016) *Third-Generation Holocaust Narratives: Memory in Memoir and Fiction*. Maryland: Lexington Books.
- Levi, P. (1991) *If This Is a Man / The Truce*. New ed. Trans. Woolf, S. London: Abacus.

Although the editor makes every effort to verify the accuracy of the information published, BrightSummaries. com accepts no responsibility for the content of this book.

www.brightsummaries.com

Ebook EAN: 9782806298614

Paperback EAN: 9782806298621

Legal Deposit: D/2017/12603/335

This guide was written with the collaboration of Florence Balthasar for the chapters 'A universal novel' and 'Personal and poetic'.

Cover: © Primento

Digital conception by Primento, the digital partner of publishers.

This guide was produced with the support of the *Service Général des Lettres et du Livre* of the Wallonia-Brussels Federation.